HOW TO SUCCEED WITH WOMEN

ANTHONY F BADALAMENTI PhD

Library of Congress Catalog Card Number 93-85891
ISBN 1-880365-90-1

Gilliland Printing, Inc.
Arkansas City, KS 67005

THIS BOOK IS DEDICATED TO THE VERY BEST IN YOUR LIFE

THIS BOOK IS DEDICATED TO THE VERY BEST IN YOUR LIFE

Preface

The pages that follow combine insight and method to help you achieve your goals as a male who wants to succeed with women. Success may mean winning the girl of your dreams for a permanent relation. It could mean becoming more proficient at meeting women, or at dating and getting to know them. You may want to better understand what a relation involves psychologically. Whatever your goals are, my objective is to stir in you those feelings and attitudes which will create your success. I also give you a great deal of practical information to help you, especially in making a first connection. Insight helps, so does action. You need both and I try to bring you to both. Nothing is more effective in life than informed action.

Two streams meet to create this book. Twenty years of work in psychiatric research contribute deep insights into the makeup of women. Fifteen years of involvement with the single lifestyle industry provides intimate knowledge of the practical problems facing the single male. The fusion of these approaches, one grounded in theory and the other in practice, results in a reliable guide for the single male who wishes to take action and to be confident of his outcome.

The material in this book has worked remarkably well for me. It has worked so well that many men have asked me to write a book about how to do it. I took up their suggestion remembering how I once wished for more from the world of the single male. If you live in that world and want more from it this book can help you. Its spirit and its practical advice will help you to succeed.

Note to the Reader: Getting the Most from This Book

It is as impossible for a man to be cheated by anyone but himself, as for a thing to be, and not to be, at the same time.

...from Compensation by Ralph Waldo Emerson

If you are earnest about wanting to do better with women then this book can change your life. It will make you conscious of women's inner make up. You will enter their world and learn how they see you. You will no longer see them as strange, difficult or inscrutable. The experience will transform your life as you work with it. It will put you in touch with your male forces that women spend their entire lives searching for. You will learn about your magical hold over them.

Exercises are given at the end of each chapter. Do them. To read this book and not do the exercises is to compromise much of its benefit. They will help you to more fully understand the material and, more importantly, to live it and to put your energy out into the world. Spend time with them. Your efforts will be rewarded at many levels.

The exercises are based on visualization techniques which have been found to be highly effective. You will be guided in visualizing along the way. It is a technique that most people enjoy and do naturally. Follow the instructions carefully and acquire skill in it. Use your own judgment and design an exercise regimen that meets your needs.

A selection of poetry or prose at the beginning of each chapter announces its mood and sense. After reading each chapter and doing the exercises, return to its beginning. Read the selection again, and let it charm you into a fuller experience of the chapter's meanings. The color of the author's words will help you take possession of their meaning.

A first reading will give you a sense of how this book empowers you to move to higher levels of success. I recommend that you reread it as necessary to continue to energize and transform yourself. Each next reading will bring you to new levels of skill in your social life and of discovery there and elsewhere.

Before you get underway I want to share with you a recent experience I had in the middle of writing this book. I was at a party talking to a very attractive woman, the sort whose demeanor tells you at once that she has a great deal to offer. Our conversation drifted to my work on this book. She asked for me some examples of the techniques which I felt work so well. I told her about a procedure that I later name the umbrella technique in this book. Her mouth and eyes opened wide as she said with a gesture of happy helplessness "My goodness! Why don't you just go and tell all our secrets"? Bon appetit!

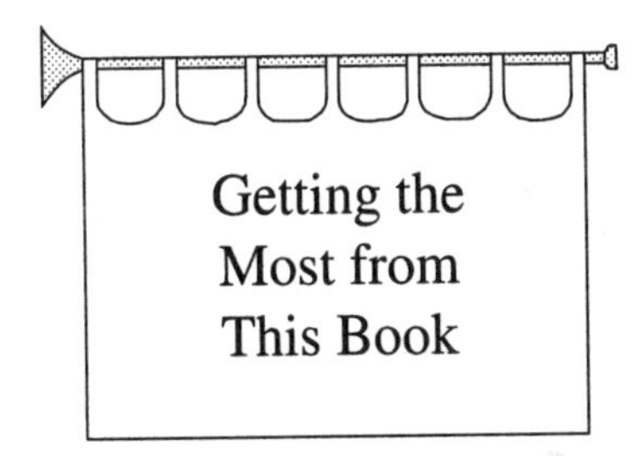
Getting the
Most from
This Book

TABLE OF CONTENTS

PART I: EXCALIBUR

Preparing for Success

PART II: CAMELOT

The Refinement of Success

EXCALIBUR
Preparing for Success

It was the sword of success and whoever used it could not be defeated. This beautiful legend has feet in reality. Part I of this book presents the means, by concept and by skill, of getting what you want. Take them into your life and work with them because they will work for you.

There is more to the legend of the sword. Whoever wore the scabbard of excalibur had proof against injury and was free to go forward again and again. That is a fine image to hold as you build to more success. Every outcome which is not entirely what you want teaches you how to get more with your next effort.

Preparing for Success

Chapter 1

What Is Really Different?

And here's the happy bounding flea—
You cannot tell the he from she.
The sexes look alike, you see;
But she can tell, and so can he.

...from the Flea by Roland Young

Most people exaggerate the differences between the sexes. They count too many things in and too few out. A man's physical and psychological experience of himself has much more in common with a woman's than otherwise. In almost every way men and women are more alike than different. Success with women depends on seeing this. Where the differences are real, they come as so many contrasts to the usual likeness, teaching new and more effective responses.

Women are more aware of these things than men are and they use their insight well. This is not new. Countless ages of nursing both sexes have sensitized them to it. The entire task of child rearing was once sent to them without question. They were taught early in their childhood that their role was in caring for the family. Their view of themselves formed around creating and upholding life. As a result their energy went to becoming more emotional and intuitive. At that early time the greater strength of the male was sent to deal with the hazards of life found in a hostile world. The male hunted, protected and developed a lore of stoutheartedness.

Obviously, each sex noticed the messages given the other and silently learned from them. That was a good idea in a world that needed to maintain the fiction of an immense gender difference. We are no longer in that world where each sex has to muffle how it also responds to the messages given to the other sex. The world is now standing up to how alike the sexes are and is being charmed into discovering the real differences.

Science verifies the likeness. The physiologies of men and women are almost identical. This is why, with little and obvious exception, medical texts present the same material for both sexes. Down to the smallest detail the differences dissolve away. For every feature which is prominent in one sex you will find its lesser image in the other sex. This is easy to see with breasts and buttocks for one, and with the pairing of a man's penis with a woman's clitoris for another. Also, when a physician diagnoses a patient, most of the inferences proceed the same for both sexes.

The experience of the inner self is similar for both sexes. A woman's hopes for her friends, family and community are very much like a man's. Her experience of the desire for satisfying work is essentially the same as a man's. She will show happiness for a job well done and anxiety over uncertainty the same way a man does. The fact is, each sex has all the inner workings of the other with differences only in their magnitudes.

You will need to become more aware of the likeness between the sexes to succeed more with women. Go to work on this. Set yourself to find something, anything, in yourself which you feel women do not experience. Then put the shoe on the other foot and see if you can find something from their inner life which you think men don't have and test it against your own experience. In the end you will discover that there are a few things, not very many, that truly divide the sexes.

Women, who always seem to know these things in the first place, welcome men who see that it is so. They respond richly to men who respect them as persons with little emphasis on sexual difference. Look for it in the next women you meet. It will make your time with them easier and more natural.

What Is Really Different?
Exercise for chapter 1

Get a piece of paper and draw a line down its center. Write on the left side all the ways in which you feel that men and women are alike and on the right side all the ways in which you see them as different. The likenesses should far exceed the differences and begin to reveal how much our culture exaggerates the sexual difference. If you have listed more differences than likenesses then redo the exercise.

What Is Really Different?

Chapter 2

An Important Difference

She walks in Beauty, like the night
Of cloudless climes and starry skies;
And all that's best of dark and bright
Meet in her aspect and her eyes;
Thus mellowed to that tender light
Which Heaven to gaudy day denies.

...from She Walks in Beauty
by George Gordon, Lord Byron

Some men contemplate women as an ultimate mystery. They stand before men as creatures of wonder holding the keys to a magical kingdom of joy and happiness. They are living promises of what can be and perhaps should be. Men follow the lines of attraction that women send out and too often find no way to connect with them at the other end. They find too little in their own masculine ways to help empathize with what women feel or value. Again and again their eyes tell them that women want them but the process of coming together miscarries. The frustrations often make women seem unreasonable and beyond comprehension.

Women's feelings on these matters are closer to men's than men usually think. Women are also frustrated, disappointed and wonder where and how to place their efforts. They have a sharper sense of where things go wrong, from their point of view, than men. That is, women are clear on where they did not get what they want and men are unclear about what went wrong in the first place. They are usually quite specific about their discontent with men.

Many key differences between the sexes are unperceived and subtle. Knowing them positions you for success. Some of the not so noted differences are emotionally attached to the striking differences in shape and form. It may often seem that nature made women for men to admire as creatures of immense physical charm. That is true but the way they want to be admired is a large concern for them. They have in mind a different model based on their attraction to the charm and beauty of men's bodies.

The emotions of physical attraction are not entirely the same for both sexes. A man will usually feel good about being admired by a woman for his physical beauty. He takes it to mean that she is keying in to his dynamism. It is not the same for women. In the opening moments of a relation, she will resent and be hurt by a man who admires her face and form over her psychological make up. It is difficult to over emphasize the importance of the last sentence; you may want to read it again. Women are beautiful and want to be seen that way. They want you as a male to discover the beauty of their emotional makeup, their psychology, and their psyche. Only after they trust that you perceive their inner, personal beauty will they welcome your appreciation of their physical beauty. Women place considerable value on their inner experience and prize it above all else. They do not want your attraction to their lines to overtake your perception of their insides. They have an almost phobic dread of being seen as no more than a sex object. Her heart's wish is that the new man in her life will begin to learn of her inner beauty by seeing how she wears it on the outside. In their own eyes the energy of their magical inner world radiates out to men through their form.

Women see themselves as expressions of nature's highest creative energy. There are great joys and much happiness waiting for the male who learns that women want men to discover the wonders of nature within them. Women experience their inner life poetically as the eternal feminine living in them. Within themselves, women do not use words to understand themselves or others. They use their extraordinarily intuitive feelings to understand events and to respond to them. They send energy with their feelings to themselves and to you. The more they love the more they send the gift of their feminine energy. And they want you as a male to sense their energy. They want you to feel the wonder and beauty of the universe in their emotional make up because that is how they see themselves and that is, in fact, how they are composed.

It is not true that the male use of logic is superior to female intuition or vice versa. Both are powers of nature and each has its own strength and purpose. Just as you as a male are drawn to what may appear to be a mysterious intuition in a female, so is the female drawn to the male power of logic, focus and purpose that is usually difficult for them to experience. It is nature's design to separately express its male and female energies in different sexes. This does not mean that women are only female and men only male. Not at all. We are both mixtures of both sexes with one gender dominating. The more you study what is feminine within you the more easily you will understand women and find joy in their company. Women are women because female energy is dominant in them and not because there is no male energy in them, and vice versa.

Women have no greater wish with men than that men should see and marvel at their radiance of their inner beauty. Women feel safe and secure when they see your male energy moving with fascination from their outer beauty to their inner world. Women trust men whom they sense want to become one with their psychological experiences. Such trust is well placed because the man who can empathize with a woman's emotions must also be in touch with himself.

When a woman is drawn to a man it is because she wants to experience the male voice of the universe. She is aware of this. She is very much in touch with herself as the female voice and tends to assume that you have a parallel awareness of yourself. A man's inner experience is to feel the might and majesty of the universe. Women know that too and their highest wish for you is to draw your power through the veil of their outer form to their inner subjective world.

Women place their security in their inside. They have an anxious awareness that their outer charms will fade. To them the inside is real and enduring. They look within for a life which never ceases to grow and become richer and more complete. It is to this world—the place of the eternal feminine—that they invite you.

An Important Difference
Exercise for chapter 2

Call to mind a sonnet or poem which you feel well describes feminine beauty. I suggest that you use something other than Byron's words given earlier. If necessary take the time to fetch a book with such material and make a selection. Focus on those word constructions which you feel capture the inner beauty of women. Look for some level of their experience in your own emotions. Now think of a woman that you favor and try to see how what you have felt in yourself is so much more true of her. In your imagination tell her what you see.

This exercise will help you to understand what women really want and how to give it to them. Work with it and take large steps to becoming more of what they want.

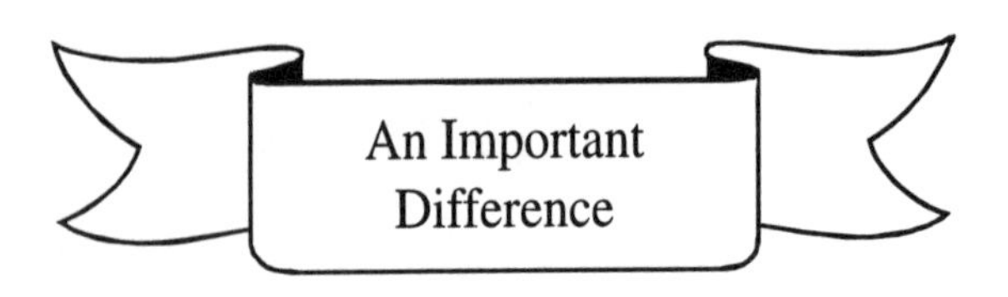
An Important
Difference

Chapter 3

How Women See Men

Lo! said Merlin, yonder is that sword that I spake of. With that they saw a damosel going upon the lake...Damosel, said Arthur, what sword is that, that yonder the arm holdeth above the water?...Sir Arthur, king, said the damosel, that sword is mine, and if ye will give me a gift when I ask it you, ye shall have it. By my faith, said Arthur, I will give you what gift ye ask. Well! said the damosel, go ye into yonder barge, and row yourself to the sword, and take it and the scabbard with you, and I will ask my gift when I see my time.

...from LeMorte D'Arthur by Sir Thomas Malory

If you think that most women have cynical perceptions of men then you are correct. Women, like men, have had too many negative experiences in relations or in social situations. And they have an inner, mental ideal of what a man should be. Your are measured against this ideal. Many women will admit, in confidence, that they want a man who is a woman in a male body. Why? Because they have considerable confidence in the ability of their own gender to understand their needs and strivings. Trust is very important to woman, much more so than to men. Women feel instinctively that they can trust one another to empathize with their feelings.

Women usually have little faith that a man—any man—can know how important their psychology is to them. They often discredit male interest as being limited to sexual desire. The less mature woman will go further and allege that men are infantile, taken up with a childish sense of power which they will refer to as male ego. Their allegations reflect a shortage of understanding on their part as to how the male is made: the male is nature's expression of the drive to creatively alter the world around us. Where women are more creative with what is personal, men act more with the basic stuff of life and the world.

When a woman first meets you she feels excited by the power of your male energy. She will be looking for signs that your eyes go within her to her soul, bringing your power with them. If you are peering into her psyche then you will feel her female energy leap out toward you; she will become unable to restrain the outflow of herself to you. However, if she is not sure that you are going within, or worse if she feels you cannot or will not look within her, then she will pause. If she becomes convinced that your attention is not going to her insides, she will then withdraw from you and continue her search for the man who understands. A woman will catalog you as a childish male, preoccupied with your own ego if she feels that your attention is limited to her looks and that you have little interest in her as a person. This is a sensitive issue with them.

On first encounters women want you to find them pretty, even sexy. But they will beat a hasty retreat from you if communicate your delight over their sexuality too much. They are very vigilant for the male who seeks their personal energy and affectionate ways first and their sexuality second. Women cannot resist giving you all the wonders of their sexuality if they see that you first want to receive the inner energy of their psyche. Savor the subjective first and you will stir an irresistible drive in them to reward you with all that they are.

Women are somewhat mysterious and they want to see that you see that they are. Your perception of their mystery creates in them a sense of trust in you. It also creates a powerful desire to be with you because they have an innate need to be seen. In my opinion, few men ever come to learn this and most men spend too much of their lives scratching their heads wondering what they really want. They want to be discovered, and as you will see, in more ways than one.

How Women See Men
Exercise for chapter 3

Think of two opposite situations you have seen or experienced socially. In one a woman responds warmly and with welcome to a fellow. In the other, she is put off and withdraws. Form a mental image of yourself literally stepping into her and therefore taking on her inner experience. Do this for each of the two situations and concentrate on the emotions she is feeling within herself. Note what she is seeing in the man before her. What happens differently within her when she is with the man she welcomes as opposed to the man she withdraws from?

Now form a mental image of a woman you want to meet or get to know. See yourself step into her experience as you approach her. What does she want to see in you and what does she not want to see? Feel her expectations and hopes. By stepping into what she wants you not only rehearse success but also move toward personal growth into the better ways of being and living which assure it.

Chapter 4

What Do Women Want in Relationships?

Art! Who comprehends her?
With whom can one consult
concerning this great goddess?

...from a letter by Ludwig van Beethoven

It is true that women are instinctively more monogamous than men. This is a source of despair in women, often driving them to resign themselves to the idea of never finding a faithful partner. Most women never fully give up this fear in the back of their minds when they enter a committed relation. So why then do they commit?

Women do not want to be discovered only in the moments of your first encounter with them. They want the process to be ongoing, and in many ways. It gives them a deep joy and satisfaction to know that you are with them in spirit and that you value what they value. However, women are extraordinarily generous in relations. Most are willing to give more of themselves than men are. The drive to nourish and to create the personality of the other is stronger in the female than in the male. This is the root of their generosity.

When a women decides to enter a relation she expects at least two things. One is that the fellow she cares for will continue to submerge himself in her mystery. The other is to light up his life by giving herself to his ongoing growth. Women are never happier than when they feel that they can fulfill the man they trust. It is their intention to give themselves fully to that end and they hope that you will abide by it.

More than men, women become fulfilled by fulfilling. This is a principle of nature. The drive to find joy this way is so strong that it drives the deep fear of infidelity into the background. More than that, most women feel that in giving enough of their creative energy to the man they love, they will secure his love against all others. Men who violate this cause women more pain than they probably know and women never forget such violations of their trust.

Women, like men seek a relation for the usual good things such as love, affection, emotional support, possibly a family, a shared life, and so on. However, they see these things as outcomes rather than as goals and men see them as goals rather than as outcomes. To women, these ordinary good things are among the results of being with a man they trust and honor by giving themselves to him. They see themselves as the psychological cause of the good things they want to obtain.

Every woman has a deep hope that the man she cares for will become more and more intrigued with her personality. They look to put men under the spell of their energy, knowing instinctively that men become intoxicated by it. One of the great goods of a relation for them is the promise that the male will ever after be charmed by her inner life. Poets and painters have known this for ages. This is why so many of the world's great work of art present women as inscrutably beautiful.

The next time you are at an art museum note the paintings of women made by men versus those made by women. They will emphasize different aspects of the feminine. Male artists paint the beauty, warmth and seductive charm of women. The female artists give you images of how they send sublime love to those they care for, revealing how they see themselves as givers of life.

What Do Women Want in Relationships? Exercise for chapter 4

Part I. Draw a line down the middle of a sheet of paper. Write on one side those things you would seek in a relation with a woman. Now visualize a woman you would like to have a relation with. If there is no such person in your life now then imagine your ideal. Write on the other side those things that she would seek in a relation. Turn the paper over.

Now step into the form of the woman you are visualizing as in the prior exercise. Feel her being, her drives and intuitive desires. Hold the states you enter and repeat the exercise. When you are finished compare the two sides of the paper. If you do not find significant differences between the two sides then repeat the exercise until your visualization brings about a change.

Part II. Hold the state of part I or recreate it as above in part I. Reread the passage from the beginning of chapter 3 about Arthur, Merlin and the lady of the lake who leads him to excalibur. In that state go to the material in the passage quoted. Answer for her how it announces what she wants of you in a relation. Be sure that you are looking at the quotation through her eyes.

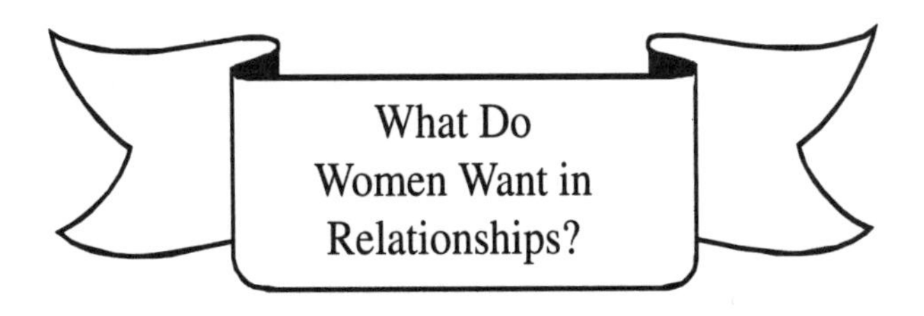
What Do
Women Want in
Relationships?

Chapter 5

Flirting: The First Encounter

Had I not walked without an upward look
Of caution under stars that very well
Might not have missed me when they shot and fell?
It was a risk I had to take—and took.

...from Bravado by Robert Frost

Flirting is remarkably easy, much more so than most people of either sex ever realize. At the heart of a good flirtation is a public statement that you feel good about her. Authenticity, some mirth and merriment, and feeling good about yourself all help. The key however to flirting is in the public announcement made by your actions that you think she is very, very nice—so nice that you risk rejection, failure and embarrassment for her sake. Women love that. And the better you feel about yourself, the more they love it and feed off of it.

This is why most women like to dance. Women see dancing as a public statement on your part of how desirable and exciting you find them, and because it is public, it is socially acceptable. When you dance with a women she usually interprets it unconsciously to mean that you esteem yourself and are therefore trustworthy. In their eyes it takes some chutzpa for a man to be expressive in public. That is why it provokes trusting admiration from them. Dancing has been called fore foreplay. Whoever said that knew what he/ she was talking about. Dancing with a women releases social inhibition in her about the propriety of being with you. True, the rhythm of the music is seductive. However, its major effect lies in releasing her from social criticism over being with you. When you dance with her you are going through an age old ritual that says you lay just claim to her and you better believe that she sees this meaning in it, however unconscious it may be.

It is tactically wise to flirt where others are present. The more you show willingness to take risks for her sake, the more she will admire you and begin to see you as trustworthy. If you are at a dance or party it is wiser to first chat with her. Dancing is a form of bonding which should follow the preliminaries of having a good initial feeling about each other. Your goals will be well served by learning to communicate to her non-verbally that you are looking for the good stuff in her as a person. She will respond to that and will want very much to dance with you no matter how much of a klutz you are on your feet. In fact, the more awkward you are—while feeling good about yourself—the more she will look up to you and be driven to give you her energy. Women do not like men who feel sorry for themselves or who are pathetic. They crave your strength but not your "machoness".

On first encounter they will be looking for how much they can trust in your male powers to support their emotions. This means that you as a male in good standing make them feel more secure about themselves just as they do something wonderfully chemical to your male emotions. It helps, but is not essential, to be creative when flirting. Being capricious and playful from a position of inner strength and confidence is very appealing to women—even to men. It's alright to be earnest but not dull. She wants your emotional color and she also wants to add to it by waking it up. Give her a chance to show you what she's got.

If you see in a public place, such as a store or library, a woman who interests you take some discreet measures to get her to note your interest. No woman can resist being found attractive, especially when you are attracted to her wining ways. Women will respect you for being daring enough to break with convention and to approach them where it may not be strictly appropriate. And they will meet you half way as long as you continue to take the initiative. They will meet you half way because they want to see if you are as intriguing to them as you apparently find them. They want to connect as much as you do.

You could begin with a smile and a statement such as "I think you are very attractive". It pays to be honest, direct and a little daring because that will elicit a favorable response, usually of delighted admiration for your willingness to try your luck. You can be a little more creative and deliberately bump your carriage – gently – into hers and then comment with a smile "I'm glad you are in my way" or better "Are you in my way?". She will smile and wait for you to say something else. Say anything. It won't matter. She will be under the spell of a male who dares to take chances because he finds her attractive. You can suggest playfully "let's talk about this while we shop together". Be capricious and go for it!

Sometimes there are second and third opportunities with a woman that you want to get to know. This can occur, for example, if she happens to live near you or if she frequents the same places as you and so on. Persistence pays in the matter of a woman's affection. It has often been said that a man can make a woman fall in love with him but a woman cannot make a man do so with her. The feminine need to be discovered and wanted is so basic that very often second or later attempts win their interest after a few unsuccessful forays. The idea of persistence paying is true with them because they so much value your perception of them as worthwhile and beautiful. Your persistence also makes them feel that they can trust you, and at several levels.

Flirting: The First Encounter
Exercise for chapter 5

Think of a recent time when you saw two people flirting with each other. Recall it vividly so that you see all the details and movements. Step into the woman and visualize what she sees and experiences. Draw upon your recollection to make this accurate. Now what do you feel she perceived as being done "right" and what do you feel she wished he would have done but did not? Remember, she wants to be found attractive, desirable and interesting by a fellow who feels good enough about himself to take chances for her sake. She wants to be discovered by a man's inner strength.

Flirting: The
First Encounter

Chapter 6

Finesse in Flirting: The Umbrella Technique

Afoot and light-hearted I take to the open road,
Healthy, free, the world before me,
The long brown path before me,
leading wherever I choose...
Henceforth I ask not good-fortune,
I myself am good-fortune.

...from Song of the Open Road by Walt Whitman

It is in the nature of masculine ways to want to move quickly and aggressively to its objects. Getting to the target and winning are true signs of male energy. I have included this chapter to satisfy that urge. Some of you will want to go faster and higher. Much has been written about what to do after you make an initial connection—whether in your social or work life. But everyone knows that the real difficulty is in getting started. That first push on the bicycle pedal can be strenuous and long.

You may have sensed in the last chapter that women have certain surface traits in their emotional make up which they want you to appeal to. It pays to be upbeat and to feel good about yourself. They want to see these things and to feel your energy. There are more specific ways you can do this. Two interesting chance events some years ago—I think it was 1979—made me realize that I was using them.

I was at a tennis party with a woman I was then dating. Call her Susan. She drew me into a conversation about the male social life and began to tease me about what a flirt I was. I responded by relating that my interest in women was sincere and grounded in the most healthy drives men can have. She agreed with this and drew me more deeply into how I flirt. By the way, Susan was herself a very accomplished flirt of the other gender. We began to discuss the art and science of flirting—this was not an entirely tongue in cheek conversation.

I offered the idea that she appealed to the basic need of all males to be found desirable because of their strength, robustness and ability to be directed. Susan said she knew that. And then she converged rapidly on me and said "What woman would not want to be with you when you make her feel like she's the only woman in the room". The quoting is accurate. You see I was so taken by the simple, sweeping accuracy of her statement that I memorized it then and there.

Take it from a woman: make her feel like the only person there and she will adore you for it. The more people there are around you, especially other women, the better. This is more than a visual technique which requires you to keep your gaze on her. You should direct your emotional and mental attention to her to achieve this. If you are interested in her in the first place you will tend to do this anyway. By studying the technique and looking for feedback from the woman you are flirting with you will get better and better at it. It is highly effective and it feeds directly into the way they want to be appealed to. They will find it natural and easy to follow your energy.

Later that same year I was in Houston for a conference with two close male friends. We wanted to see the sights and get a sense of the locals. We loved it. The people were so friendly and the women so lovely that we did not want to leave. We naturally admired the women of Houston over dinner, from our car, on the pavement, and so on. We were sold on their ways and wanted to find some company to do Houston with.

We all set out at the same time and in the same place to try our luck. Now my natural way is very much the directed way of males—as long as there is no indiscretion, I go for what I want when I see it regardless of where it is and what is going on. In walking through one of the underground passages which connect the streets of Houston we came upon three gorgeous women. That was it, I approached them and said, with a smile and the deep focus I mentioned earlier, "Excuse me. We are visitors from New Jersey and everywhere we go in Houston we just keep finding beautiful women like you. How do you do it". Needless to say, they were thrilled and begin to meow and coo over how nice it was of us to think so and how "You really shouldn't" and "Do you really see it that way?" and "What about the gals back in New Jersey?"

The essence of this technique is to enhance the good feelings you give a woman in a flirtation. Women love your upbeat ways and your ability to channel your male strength. But they love being turned on even more. I don't mean being sexually turned on. I mean that they love it when you hurl a great deal of sweet male energy their way—they call this being swept off their feet. To do this you must keep delivering much emotional energy to them. You should be full of mirth and merriment when you do this. You should also communicate as obviously as possible how simply wonderful you feel about the chance to make their acquaintance.

With both of these more advanced techniques—making a woman feel as though you perceive only her and giving her a large dose of positive emotional energy—you should maintain the posture of a dignified gentleman. Failure to be polite and discreet will create anxiety and tension in her which you will then have to manage. Better to optimize the whole thing from the outset and approach them as a gentlemen with courtesy and respect for their person. They will also favor your keeping in the background just how seductive and sensuous you find them—but do find them such.

A few years later I had another experience that led to a method which made these skills easier and more fun to acquire. I was at a party looking out at the drizzle from the porch of my friend's home. A very attractive woman approached the house protected by an interesting umbrella. It was made of clear plastic and surrounded her upper body almost like a very large hat. I could see through it that she was very pretty. As she approached I felt a rush of mirth come over me and I said to her "Look at this—a lady in a membrane!" She broke out in laughter. We wound up in the drizzle walking and sharing her umbrella. She was delightful and the experience was wonderful.

I worked with the image of the umbrella later on. It occurred to me that the closed space of the transparent umbrella felt like being alone with her while in public. It facilitated the sense image of perceiving only her, almost as if you and she have a great invisible bubble around you. It also came to me that the sense of enclosure which the umbrella gave—where you can almost feel each others body heat—also feeds the image of giving her a great deal of your personal energy.

When I see a woman that I want to link with I often also see the transparent umbrella again. It causes a pleasant rush of feeling within me that makes the event fun and exciting—and more effective. I suggest that you bring the umbrella technique with you into the exercise below and then into your social life.

Finesse in Flirting: The Umbrella Technique
Exercise for chapter 6

Rehearse the techniques sketched here in your imagination. Recall a flirtation that you feel good about. It could be one of your own or someone else's. This exercise will be more effective if it is one of your own. Use your visualization skills to move deeply into the images and to recreate the sense perceptions of the event. Step into and relive it. Proceed to its end and then rewind it in your mind.

Now step out a moment and fill your consciousness with the two techniques of this chapter. Use the umbrella image to help you here. Go forward now with that awareness and see yourself back in the event but redoing it with these new skills. Do this several times a week and you will be well rewarded.

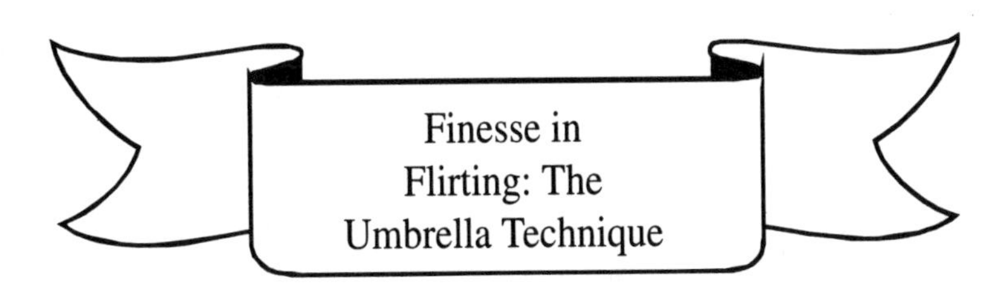
Finesse in
Flirting: The
Umbrella Technique

Chapter 7

Getting to Know Her

The meeting of two personalities is like
the contact of two chemical substances:
if there is any reaction, both are transformed.

...from Modern Man in Search of a Soul
by C. G. Jung

Successful flirting opens the door to a relation, whatever idea of one you may have in mind. The opening phase of a relation offers an opportunity for that romantic excitement which makes all the world gladly step aside. It is a time of emotional magic. True, it is transitory. But it is a thing to be enjoyed and to be done right for its own sake.

If she wants to get to know you then she has wonderful stuff in mind for you. She wants to see if you really can sense her inner life and be relied on to empathize with her experience. Sharing her subjective experience of herself is, in her eyes, the major good she has to give you. Sexual relations for her are your opportunity to enter more deeply into her as a person.

It is an event of great trust on her part to offer you herself sexually. Every time a woman offers her intimacy to someone new she feels she is taking a risk and she will be hoping for the best in the back of her mind.

The traditional gestures such as gifts of flowers or perfume tell her more than that you find her special. She will perceive these as an encoded way of telling her that you sense and favor the magic of her creative, female energy. Unconsciously she will also take this to mean that you want the nourishment of her warmth and tenderness to support your inner life.

Progress in getting to know each in the honeymoon phase is largely learning to be supported by the other's emotional life. The more you see and feel her actual beauty as a person the more successful the relation will be. This should happen by itself without effort on your part. If you find yourself struggling to see these things then you probably have not selected a woman who is right for you. It would then be a good idea to also reexamine your objectives.

If the choice is right you will find yourselves feeding off of each other. You will find her interesting, sexy, creative and fun to be with. You will look to her for vision and support in your own life. She will seek and find security in your greater male willingness to take chances and to focus your energy. You will naturally select different areas for leadership with each other and you will both be happy with those choices. Joint leadership will arise in those many areas where the sexual difference vanishes.

Poets have recognized for centuries that nature expresses its eternal feminine in women. They have spun the idea beautifully in rhymes and lyrics and have been faithful to what the eternal feminine is. As you move into and past the honeymoon phase you will know if you are contacting and being touched by this ineffable beauty in her. How will you know? You will fall for her. You will fall because it is difficult to stop your inner life from leaping out of you to meet the offer of what she is. You might even fall big time, as they say, and fall in love with her. Love is one of the natural healthy outcomes in the male of seeing this wonder in the woman. And she knows that better than you do. That is why women are so, so good at waiting. Deep within they know that there is a very good chance you will eventually be smitten by what they know they have within themselves.

If love is not your objective you should probably take time out to think over what you really want. If your current interests are basically to enjoy life more with no prospect of commitment then you should be aware of what nature might have in store for you. However, if you are not ready for a committed relation then rest easy—it is not then in nature's power for you to be so smitten by her that you will want it. You may have no more than a healthy wish to want to sample different personalities while learning more of life. Go forward and enjoy yourself. Someday, when both you and nature want it, you will find yourself captivated by her.

Getting to Know Her
Exercise for chapter 7

This exercise will help you find what your objectives are at this time. Visualize the woman you would like to meet and get to know. Put her into a concrete physical image. See before you a path which leads to where your feelings want to go. Begin to walk with her along that path. As you do take careful note of what you see and of how far you go. Listen to the dialogue in your image. Be vigilant for anything which stirs anxiety or creates discomfort as you visualize your stroll together.

When you feel like stopping take note of where you are. Is it a crowded urban area, meaning that you probably seek adventure and experience more than anything else. Or is it a quiet and lovely country setting, suggesting that you want a close and committed relation. Look carefully at your images and how you feel when you return to the present moment. Sift through them until they tell you what you want now.

Chapter 8

Endings and Beginnings

No sooner met, but they looked;
no sooner looked but they loved;
no sooner loved but they sighed;
no sooner sighed but they asked one another the reason;
no sooner knew the reason they sought the remedy.

...from As You Like It by William Shakespeare

The end of a relation is not a happy time especially if there are many good times to look back on. The up side of ending is that it offers the opportunity for you do better than ever before. You can also learn how to make yourself more desirable to women than ever before. The sense of hurt that you are likely to feel at this time can hold you up. It is therefore wise to deal with it first.

Where there is hurt there is anger as well as some other negative feelings. Wait for the negative emotions to cool down and then call or write her. Be positive with yourself and her by revealing that your are committed to a higher purpose. Remind her of how you prospered together and of the good things that you shared. Let her know that you will carry these good images with you as you go forward. She will want to hear this for several reasons. A woman does not want to feel that she has so hurt you as to anger and impair you. It will relieve her to know that you are well, fine and moving on. She will feel acquitted, so to speak. She also will respect and admire you for communicating good will to her as well as your intent to lead a happy, rewarding life.

It is important to sincerely feel this way toward her. Why do this, you may wonder, if you probably will have no further major contact with her? Women do not want to pity men. They want to admire men who rise above their wounds—they see this as the magic of masculine energy. They are taken with a number of heroic ideals as fitting for men. You will also want to go forward in life with a happy, inner sense of knowing that she supports you as a person. This will give you an uplifting sense of the memory. She will want this from you too. There is little to gain in trying to go forward with the baggage of resentment.

The next woman you meet will intuitively sense how the last relation ended. That next woman will want to see higher ideals in you. She will want to respect and admire the way you released each other from your last involvement with well wishing and grace. By ending with good will and mutual support you not only make your life easier in all that you do, but more, you are building within yourself the trustworthiness that women so much want to see in men.

When the end has come and you look back you can only account for yourself. This means that you can only be sure of what did not work for you. You can only speculate as to how she feels about it. Here is an opportunity for you to take large steps forward. Look back on the relation from her point of view as a woman and try to see what made her less than satisfied. Did you, for example, come to a point where you no longer found her inner world engaging and beautiful? Did she come to feel that she could not effectively support you and your life? Both of these wishes—to be discovered as wondrous and to support the man they care for—are of fundamental importance to women. Perhaps she felt that you were not as proud of her as person as she wanted. Women very much want you to see their worth as persons—this is one core issue where men and women are very similar. When you fail to acknowledge their worth as persons, they will think of you as sexist and become anxious that your esteem for them is poorly grounded.

You will know when your speculations have drawn you to the real issues. A sense of conviction and the "aha" feeling will come over you to tell you that you are on the right track. These discoveries are wonderful gains for you because as you see them you will become sensitized to how to do better next time. You will see how to get more of the good things that you want. You will not even have to work at it. Your own healthy desire for a good relation will give you all the energy you need to go further in the areas you now see. When the real issues come upon you so does the better way.

You may be tempted to call your former mate when you feel you have found what the problems were. I do not mean calling to resume the relation—that is up to you. If it is over, it is usually not wise to call and check in on these matters. Discussing your insights with her involves a downside risk. She could easily feel that if she had more in some sense then things would have turned out differently. Why risk hurting someone, especially someone you shared an important part of your life with? Better to go forward with quiet but potent insight preparing you for happier and more effective action next time.

Endings and Beginnings
Exercise for chapter 8

Carry out the suggestions of this chapter. Recall a former relation, preferably your last one. Use your visualization skills to recreate it as fully as possible. See the colors, the details and the places you frequented. Hear the sounds and voices. Feel the textures and surfaces that were there. Step into it live so that you no longer are looking at it but are in it. Now experience the scenario as it unfolds. Work with the images to more fully understand what happened. This will help you to find ways to make your next relation better and more fulfilling.

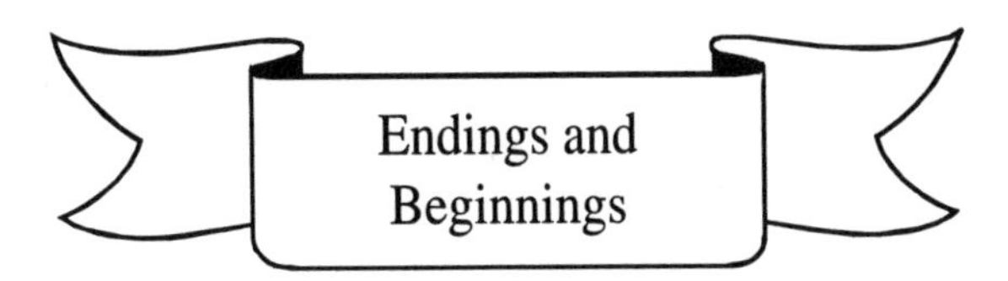
Endings and
Beginnings

Chapter 9

Starting Fresh

He only earns his freedom and existence
who daily conquers them anew...
The Eternal Feminine draws us on.

...from The Gothic Chamber
by Johann Wolfgang von Goethe

If you are not now in a relation then, in some sense, you starting anew after the last one. Usually it is a good idea to not rush from one relation to another. Take some time to reflect as outlined in the last chapter. You will easily know when you are ready because you will feel restless and too solitary. If all else escapes your notice, your chemistry will tell you.

The key to more success is to not only want more from the next relation, but to demand it of life. Highly successful people often say that you have to make life pay your price. Their advice is well worth noting. Reviewing the events and problems of your prior relations works you into a state where you can better give yourself to the next one. That is one reason why it is fitting to also expect more.

As you move about in your life let your consciousness drift freely to your prior involvements. Live with them and let them speak to you. They will tell you what sense there was in the many meanings of your emotional responses to the women you were drawn to. The meanings that you value tell you where to go to get more the next time. The others may tell you, among other things, when and why you are being drawn to the wrong ones. This process will help you chart your course. It will also give you a practical understanding of the positions of the male and female in nature.

As your comprehension of female make up deepens, you will begin to see that all of nature has male and female aspects, not just human affairs. Our use of languages, and more generally of symbols, captures this well. In most languages the gender of the Sun is masculine and the moon feminine. Also, the Sun is a male symbol and the moon female in most myths. Think about that. The Sun, which represents immense power, is a male symbol. The moon, which lights the night and therefore represents unconscious illumination, is feminine. Put differently, the dynamism of the male as an effective power source is represented by the Sun, and the mystic intuitions of the female by the moon.

Shortly before writing this book I had a privileged experience on the male/female difference which I would like to share with you. It's a little philosophical but very rich in practical meanings that can make life better. I had done some reading on the Eastern ideas of yin and yang, the feminine and masculine principles of nature. A Chinese friend of mine showed me the oriental characters for yin and yang. I had to stare at them for quite a while before I saw the small and subtle differences between them. He told me that those wee differences represented the symbol of the moon for yin and of the sun for yang. I felt honored to watch him sketch a pearl of age old wisdom. It told me how long the human race has known that nature put all the answers in everyone by putting some of each sex in the other.

As your perception of the male and female energies of the universe grows, so will your joy and satisfaction in relations with women—and men! As you go forward, informed by your prior experiences, you can expect your present levels of awareness and readiness for action to continue to grow. As a rule of thumb it is not wise to expect fresh insight or fundamental changes in personal style when you are still consolidating prior gains.

Savor the process of your prior relations feeding you good things whose sense will come to closure in the near future. Look for a woman who will light up your life and who will want to share your goals. Get into the swim of the relation. In time the new relation will provide you with fresh material to finish processing your former ones. The new relation acting on your old experiences will fuel a deepening of your insight and an expansion of your awareness. This will do more than just make you feel good. It will make your personal style more graceful and your presence more charming. You will succeed more and be happier.

As noted, women have a stronger need to place their trust in their mate than men do. You can deepen this trust by sharing with her the movements of your inner experience. If you want to understand more of yourself—or of her—tell her. She will be eager to help you because her feminine make up is closer to the intuitive meaning of the psyche than your male make up; she will also like to help simply because she is a woman. She will feel good about your openness and she will unconsciously feel that you are accepting your own feminine side as well as getting closer to the magic of her own feminine soul. In time she will want to learn more about the male principle through you. As her trust deepens she will want you to share more and more of your inner experience as a male. You can go forward together.

Starting Fresh
Exercise for chapter 9

Picture yourself on a flat field. To your left is a valley and to your right the land rises up. When you look to your left you see your immediate past. As your eyes come upon the flat field you see the present. When you look to the right you see what you are becoming and what you are now consolidating.

Close your eyes and step into this image. Rather than seeing yourself at a distance, go into the scene and be a part of it. As you do this you will feel a sense of your history when you gaze from the left to the center and a sense of life's promise as you peer to the right. When you feel enough of a sense of uplifting and good expectation open your eyes and return to the present. See yourself sending these images into the world with your actions.

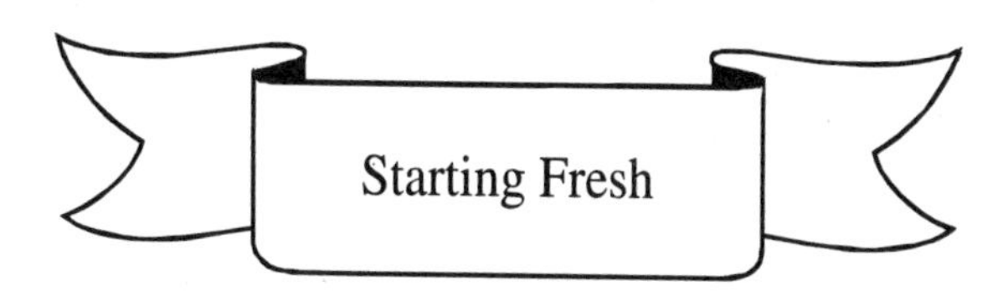

Chapter 10

Irresistible Men

What a piece of work is man!
How noble in reason!
how infinite in faculty!
in form, in moving, how express and admirable!
in action how like an angel!
in apprehension how like a god!

...from Hamlet by William Shakespeare

There are some men who seem to have an irresistible power of attraction for women. It appears that before them women have no option but to surrender to an invisible and overwhelming force. You will find some men like this in the public eye, such as political leaders, actors and athletes. Most are known only to those who share the same part of life as they do. As for the first group—those in the public eye—women perceive them as incarnations of their highest male ideal. They cannot help doing that. And you should not be envious. Women usually want no more than a passing tryst with such figures. Their dominant psychology which longs for discovery, trust and supporting the other soon pulls them back to their stable inner longings.

The second group—irresistible men not in the public eye—is more interesting and is also a richer source of insight. It is a diverse group. Among the men who are highly attractive to women are those with a basic animal magnetism. However, many of this kind are without a distinctive animal magnetism. And so magnetism is not a core issue. All such men do have an instinct to appeal to their deep inner needs as women. However, so do men who don't do as well and therefore such appealing to them is not at the heart of being irresistible.

The key difference between doing well and doing very well is found in the idea of authenticity. Women respond to the real you. The more real you are, the more they will feel secure about sending their energy to you (because they will unconsciously have confidence that their energy will be efficacious). Authenticity is more than honesty. It includes the ability to freely and happily express who and what you are. Women respond richly and automatically to authenticity—so do men. However, women see it more as a signal to trust and men more as a sign of dynamism and personal vigor.

Authenticity and self esteem go together. It is not psychologically possible to have such a free, expressive and open access to your inner self unless you can accept it as good. When you accept enough of yourself as good you are in a state of high self esteem. It is a psychological state that both sexes find compelling. Women have the highest regard for men who have such a feeling for themselves and they take authenticity as its natural expression. They are right in doing so.

There is such a thing as charm, sexual or otherwise. When a woman says that she finds a man to be charming she is telling you a few things all at once. Her smallest meaning is that he is getting to her. Her larger meaning runs in a few directions at once. It is that she sees this man as welcoming her sexuality as a good and wholesome thing, inseparable from her emotional color and her diverse psychic interior. She is also saying that he responds to her cues for acknowledgment with appropriate grace and gesture. That is why a continental kiss on the hand—when done authentically—goes so far. To a woman it is a statement that not only is she sexy and beautiful but she is also to be honored and revered as a person. Try it and see.

You can develop charm. At bottom, it is an advanced form of authenticity. You can develop authenticity if you are interested in higher levels of fulfillment. How do you do that? You do it by going out into the world and learning to enjoy more activities and interests. You do it by trying to be honest with yourself and others in order to deepen your contact with yourself. As for charm itself—the more evolved and expressive part of authenticity—it helps to read poetry, watch movies where it is acted out and to study it in others. The very serious student may want to take lessons in dancing and other art forms and to spend time in the environments of performers and artists.

You will not be able to appear or actually be more authentic until your self experience is open and real enough. You cannot fake charm as you cannot fake honesty. A fuller and more zesty plunge into life will put you in touch with more of yourself and of nature. This will breed authenticity and exposure to the arts will create charm. Do it with someone you like.

When a woman says that a man gives off a good feeling she doesn't usually mean that he has a good sense of humor. She means that she finds him charming. Humor can be part of charm but it can also be found without charm. Women, and men, are not generally amused by the cynical humor of people who attack and disparage others. There is little that is charming in such behavior. When humor makes light of what is unwelcome, thus making it less distressing and more manageable, it becomes charm. The highest use of humorous charm in flirting is to introduce wit and whimsy to dispel the tension of those moments of first encounter. Women glow over that and they will love you for it.

You will not need unusual authenticity or any significant skill with charm or humor to achieve success with your goals. Nature does not ask us to be professional in caring about one another. You don't need these skills unless you have a yen to polish yourself to the level of an art form or have a professional need to do so, as do artists and performers. It is worth while to be aware of the highest level of accomplishment because such awareness makes your actions so much easier and helps you to understand them.

Irresistible Men
Exercise for chapter 10

Turn your thoughts out to life and recall episodes where you encountered authenticity, charm or humor in social settings. Use your visualization skills. Study what you see and draw it in. Do this until it awakens pleasant emotions in you. Go to your feelings and learn what they signify to you. Hold the images and meanings they awaken in you. Repeat this and try to see what they mean to women. If you want to deepen your authenticity or develop some skill with charm or humor, repeat this exercise several times a week. The inclination to use and to form these skills will then work its way into you. You can develop charm and humor if you want to.

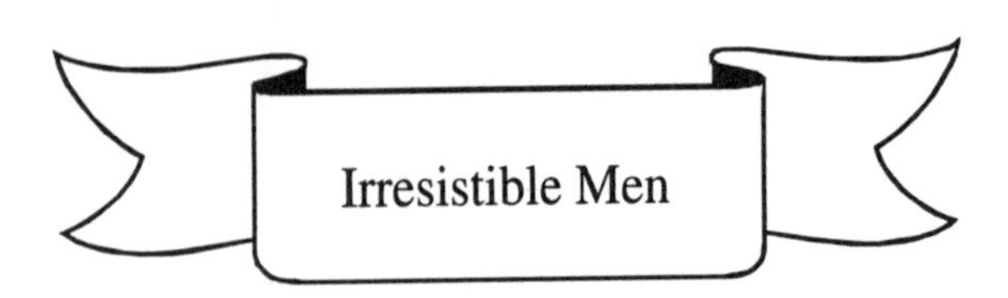

Chapter 11

The Darker Side of Women

Heaven has no rage like love to hatred turned,
Nor hell a fury like a woman scorned.

...from The Mourning Bride by William Congreve

The female of the species is more deadly than the male.

...from The Female of the Species by Rudyard Kipling

You may be wondering why this chapter is introduced with two quotations while all the others have only one. It is to emphasize the power of the dark side of woman's nature. You have read here about the presence of nature within them bestowing them with intuitions and beauty past those given to the male. The issue of their need to trust and give themselves to the support of others has been worked a number of ways. These things stand behind a logic of sorts for how impassioned an angry woman can be. The logic is that one who needs to give so much has no choice but to create a position of great vulnerability for herself.

Women invest themselves in relations more fervently than men. Their make up is more monogamous; their biology and their part of human history has made it so. One who would send so much goodness to a man becomes one who would send so much wrath to the man who trifles with her offer. It will probably surprise most men to hear that a women's need to be seen as sexy or seductive has little to do with their anger when it comes. Their inner wishes and needs are entirely grown from their innate need to give life through love and to be seen as one who does so. Women expect men to support this in them and when they decide that a man is trustworthy it is because they feel that he will do so.

Deceit and deception are among the least favored words in a woman's vocabulary. Women associate those words with the emotion of humiliation which is more painful for them than for men. If a woman comes to realize that a man has manipulated her for sexual pleasure her major resentment will not be over being exploited but over being humiliated. There is such a thing as female pride and male insincerety will flush it out. Men don't like to feel weak or ineffective. Women do not want to feel that their dignity has been compromised. Women deal with weakness better than men and men deal with injured pride better than women.

There are things more hurtful to a woman than being humiliated. They are found among the forces that work against the meaning of her nature. Men who would devote their powers to thwarting a woman's purpose are flirting with a greater and darker fury than they are likely to imagine. At the heart of her purpose are creative love supported by her intuition and a strong sense of commitment. This position is so deep in women that most would rather lose their life than the beauty of their creative purpose.

Women want men to use their power to work with them. In doing this a man becomes one of the objects and purposes of her creativity. She will want you to join her inner movements in doing this. She wants to live with quiet trust in you. She has a need to be confident that your male powers join her female purposes and submit to their objects. A woman's tendency to be possessive is one of the stronger expressions of this.

On the up side, the strength of a woman's ire reveals how very much she has to give and how very much she wants to give. Caveats have their place in life but the good stuff is found by following the energy of your higher purpose. Go with the natural and wholesome instinct to be with them for the good of their company. Your authenticity will draw the good that you want and safeguard you from the nastiness of a dark energy.

The Darker Side of Women
Exercise for chapter 11

Part I. Recall some real events and some fictitious ones, such as movies or books, where you can see the depth and strength of a woman's purpose. Spend enough time with their images to feel an emotional response to them. Put these to one side of your awareness. Now do the same thing with material that reveals the power of your own purpose, however you see it. When you have come to some emotional pitch over these things hold the feeling and step out of the images. Try to put that strength of feeling into the images you started with about woman's purpose. This exercise will create more empathy in you for the strength of the wishes they hold for you.

The Darker Side
of Women

Part II. You are about to move on to the next part of this book. Breathe deeply to clear your energy. For a few minutes think of nothing but your own breathing. When you no longer feel connected to your feelings of a few minutes ago, go to the next page.

END PART I

In the next part you will take finer and finer looks at some of the outstanding differences between the sexes and learn the skills which they support. Before you move on I recommend that you redo the exercise at the end of chapter 1. This will renew your sense of how much alike the sexes are and make you more perceptive of the differences that are really there. It will also center your judgment and give you more balance as you go forward.

PART II

Camelot
The Refinement of Success

In time the figure of Arthur became charismatic for rewarding wisdom and virtue. Men came to Camelot to be acknowledged for the merit of their works and to be rewarded for them. The charms and potent spells of Merlin empowered Arthur and excalibur to be ever victorious. Those who shared Arthur's might and Merlin's wisdom also shared the rewards.

Success is its own reward and the more of it the better. PART II gives you powerful seasoning for your knowledge and skill. Here is material to make you more effective in more circumstances. With it you will grow in grace and become poised for more effective action. These are higher levels of awareness for going further with less effort and more joy.

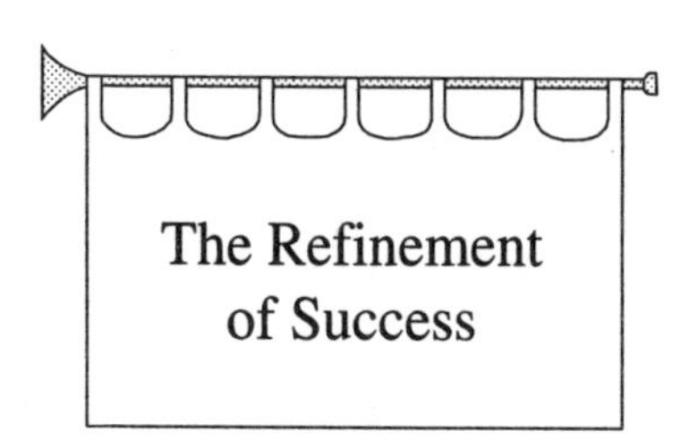

Chapter 12

The Lure of the Knight

There looms, large, uncertain, dim but glittering, the legend of King Arthur and the Knights of the Round Table...It is all true, or it ought to be; and more and better besides.

...from The Birth of Britain by Winston S. Churchill

The age of chivalry will never die because it will always live in the hearts of women. The very idea of chivalry feeds the pride they take in their beauty and the way they feel their dignity rooted in the universe itself. And you had better notice it! In their souls is the hope of an ideal man to whom they long to give everything. That ideal man is found in mature interpretation of the figure of the knight.

There are many keys to their hearts and perhaps the best among them is trust. They are enchanting creatures of immense pride and they will not risk injured pride lightly. They will forestall you at the gates until they sense that you merit their trust. And who is more trustworthy than the one who will takes chances and flirt with danger for her sake? They have taken to their hearts the idea that discretion is the better part of valor.

There is good reason for women to admire the door-holding man or the fellow who offers to help her with her packages. They are seen unconsciously as continuous with an earlier time where this meant that you offered to be their champion. The gleam of admiration flashing in her eyes when you offer her assistance is saying that she accepts you as protector of her person and her honor. It also means that she plans to reward you for your exertions. To her, you are valorous when you send your strength to the goodness of her designs which, incidentally, includes you.

Courtesy to a woman carries a similar meaning. It tells her that you esteem her person in your eyes and, in hers, it also means that you will act to uphold the dignity and worth that you see in her. They unconsciously see courtesy in a man as a thing which their psyche has created. They treasure how this as their handiwork makes them feel. To them it is also a constructive message telling others how she wants to be treated. These are all other levels of perceived and felt meaning to women when you dance with them.

It is natural to feel that the one who would defend you and uphold you against others will never hurt you. The acts of courtesy and respect shown to a woman build a sense of trust in her that you will always work with her and be good to her. Again, it is not merely fear of rejection which speaks from the back of their minds, it is the greater fear of humiliation and the potential for injured pride. The better you are to them, the more they feel satisfied that they have awakened and nurtured the goodness within you.

Every woman has to deal with how vulnerable she would feel if she committed to a lasting relation. However independent and self sufficient she may become financially, her dependency on the man's reliability will continue to distress her and cause anxiety. The metaphor of the knight has come to capture and symbolize the man who would be ideal in light of her apprehensions. The more she trusts that you honor her person and her purpose, the more she will give herself to you. It is easy to mistake her background concerns and their stress signs for PMS or other objective things. Try to be clear on which is which because they call for different affections from you. Call it right and she will desire you more and more.

The figure of the knight portrays remarkably well how male energy can drive women crazy. They see him as romantic, dashing, sexy and gallant. They see in it the stuff which promises and guarantees that they can trust the man who is getting to her. They want to feel that they are creating in you the wish to offer to worthwhile ends the strength and power which men see in it. It is a breathtaking symbol for both sexes and tells the male a great deal on how to get the good things in life. The message is not in the archaic figure of the warrior, whose destructive imagery turns women off, but in the knight's devotion to upholding decency—not just women's but everyone's.

The Lure of the Knight
Exercise for chapter 12

Go through several days of your life with a mental note to find some modern analogues of the knight. Some are easy to come upon such as police and fire fighters. There are many more and not by profession alone. Be prepared to consciously see how circumstance brings out the knight in yourself and others. At those moments turn your attention to whatever women are there, regardless of their age or composition. Look for how they well up with admiration for the figure of the knight and how they are drawn to it. At those moments recall why they respond as they do.

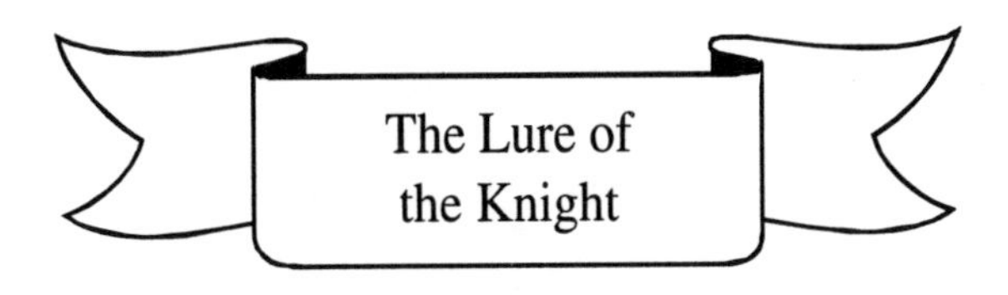

Chapter 13

Dates, Mates and More

In Xanadu did Kubla Khan
A stately pleasure dome decree:
Where Alph, the sacred river, ran
Through caverns measureless to man
Down to a sunless sea.
So twice five miles of fertile ground
With walls and towers were girdled round.

...from Kubla Kahn by Samuel Taylor Coleridge

Fresh opportunities open to you as you learn to move closer to the psychology behind women's strivings. Your better awareness increases your social skills and they, in turn, put effectiveness into your actions. You will see that many more things are now available to you that you once passed by without note. As you to get what you want, you will need to study if you want what you get. This is a different, but welcome, kind of a problem.

There are basically three types of relations to have with women. You can date them, usually for fun. You can prospect for a mate or some version of a deeper relation. Or you can be with them for prospective purposes, such as learning. There is every variety of overlap in these three categories.

Dating for fun usually begins in early youth when people are just coming out socially. It has its place everywhere in life and most people return to it at various points in life and for various reasons. People who are going through divorce, separation or the end of another form of long term committed relation usually have a need to do this. Doing so helps to keep the present issues from contaminating your next relation. The pizazz and glitter of dating for fun is a welcome change to the heavy mood that can take a hold of you at such a time. The process clears your energy, so to speak, and brings you to a state where the real meanings of your recent life come to you easily and without hurt.

Prospecting or dating for more earnest and deeper reasons comes later for most people. Sometimes fun dating evolves into a more serious relation. If your search for but persistently do not obtain a soul mate then it is time to reevaluate your objectives. It is also a time to discover some positives in the negative of not getting the outcome that you want. Is the problem with wanting or not wanting a mate or is it with a needed refinement of your judgment of who is right for you? Answering these questions tells you what you want and perhaps more importantly, who has it.

The mate search can easily become something of an education for you and that is good. You want to make a good choice. Dating for an education happens in every kind of dating relation, like it or not. We are what we are and we cannot help noting what we do. Dating to learn fits in anywhere in life and it easily merges with dating for fun. In periods of life where you feel a need to get more in touch with part of yourself or to liberate fresh strengths within, it's a good idea to date for fun and learning.

Another variety of relation is friendship. In my life I have found that women make better friends than men in some ways. I have found them to be more reliable and supportive than men and more inclined to go out of their way. They have charmed me and made me laugh with their inside take on the men in their lives—and vice versa! Friendship with a woman is guaranteed protection from hurting them for as long as you do not want her for her affections. It is not a guarantee that they will help you with your relations with other women because their competitive nature overtakes them when it comes to being found desirable.

Dates, Mates and More
Exercise for chapter 13

This exercise will help you to see how clear you on what you want and how to get it. Get a piece of paper and a pen or pencil. On the left hand side write down your goals in your relations with women. Now write down the center of the paper the qualities in women that you favor. Try to list as least as many qualities as goals. Return to the first column and place a 1 next to the goal which is most important to you, a 2 next to the runner up and so. Do likewise with the list of qualities.

Does goal 1 have a sensible relation with qualities 1 or 2? Does goal 2 have a sensible relation with qualities 2 and 3? And so on. If you find a significant amount of misalignment you may want to consider doing more of dating for fun.

Your emotional responses to this exercise are probably richer and quicker than to the one at the end of chapter 7. This exercise is a more specific version of the one given there, accommodating the greater knowledge and insight you now have.

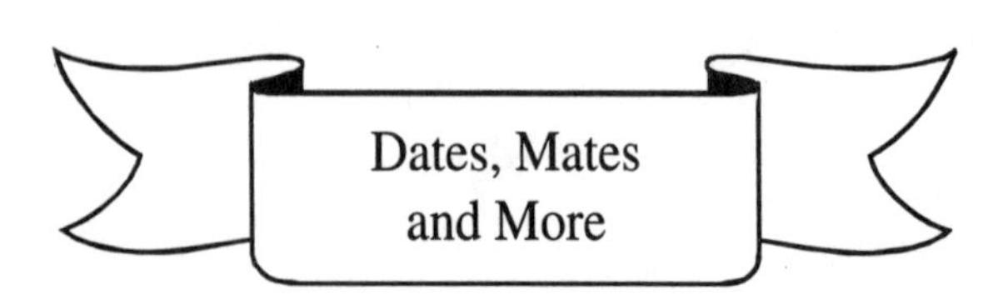

Chapter 14

The Immortal Male

O Captain! my Captain! our fearful trip is done!
The ship has weather'd every rack, the prize we sought is won,
The port is near, the bells I hear, the people all exulting.

...from O Captain! My Captain! by Walt Whitman

Men drive women just as crazy they do men. Women are just cooler about it. Being the proud creatures they are they are little inclined to say it is so, but it is. The prospect of finding a male who will complete and well order her inner experience never ceases to make them glow with hope and happy expectation. They admire the way a male can direct his strengths with focus and deliberation. They salute and send their hearts to the male capacity to clear obstacles in the path of success.

It is for the male to take chances and even to live dangerously on the path to achieving their goals. Women envy this in men. They are given to taking secure paths to their goals and are usually unwilling to take chances. When they say that men make them feel secure one of their truest meanings is that men release them from the need for taking risks. The release can be literal, where a man actually takes the risk himself for her sake. It is more often symbolic, with his presence creating in her the strength to live a little "dangerously." It is a form of emotional support. The exaggerated form of the male way—the warrior—does not appeal to them although they are thrilled by its image in fiction and the performing arts. They want to see the male principle applied to good ends and they cannot help being drawn to the male who does so.

It is inherent in male energy to change the world. The male way moves more quickly and effectively to its goals, a thing which woman find breathtaking. Their vision is clear on this. They cannot help but sense that their energy can be too diffuse and not well bound. The male way is the natural complement to this inner tendency. Their intuitions, which can be so robust and pervasive, can also wander off into space leaving them without form and disoriented. Many women will admit that they often feel unfocused and without clear center. It is difficult for most men to get the sense of this female event. You can grasp some of it by trying to combine the feeling of hopefulness with being confused. Or you can two select feelings, one which pulls you together and the other dividing you, such as the wish to love and being ambivalent.

You are the main event of their lives. As the female is majestic in voicing nature's beauty and sublime ways, the male is majestic in manifesting its power to order reality. If the dynamic power of the male is represented by a waterfall then the female is its mist subtly carrying life giving water and giving the rainbow to the world. The main event of her life is for your strength to frame her life giving ways with a firm sense of power and direction. Men are drawn to how ethereal women appear but they want within themselves to feel more regulated. They want you to be the captain of their ship.

Nature has put art into her chemistry by creating the two sexes. The mind of nature on this is for the distinction between them to be happily dissolved away in relationships. The coming together and mixing of male and female energies, personal or otherwise, is behind all the great events in the universe. The alchemists of medieval times seemed to know this. In their philosophy the meeting of male and female substances should result in a transformation of both, creating something new in which both participate. It is worth peering back at Jung's words, quoted at the beginning of chapter 7, which portray the ideas very well.

The Immortal Male
Exercise for chapter 14

Part I. Here is an exercise to bring you to see your own male energy. Some figures from classic mythology may help such as the Titans or the gods Apollo, Zeus, Hercules, Poseidon and Vulcan; mortals and part mortals such as Achilles, Ulysses, Hector, Jason and Agamemnon may also help. If you prefer recall the male figures in some great movies. For each figure write a few words of description. When you have done this for each figure look over your word descriptions to discover what they have in common. Use visualization and taking on their feeling states to help you. The answer is the immortal male in you.

Part II. Learn more about how your masculine energy centers a women and makes her feel secure and well oriented. Represent her as a sea ship with no captain, moving by the will of the water. Form an emotional image of what that would do to its passengers. Now go to the image of the captain. Visualize the well being that comes over the passengers when he makes his presence known. Watch their fears and concerns lift as he puts the ship right. Go into their feeling states as they put their faith in him. Now take on the states of the captain. Stay with being the captain navigating the ship. Look at the passengers' relief through his eyes.

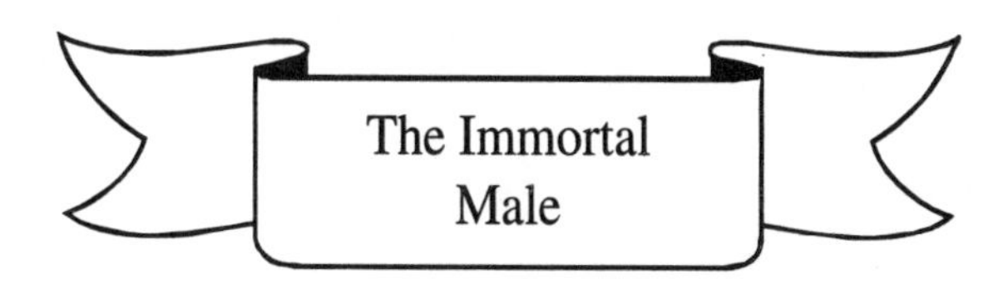

Chapter 15

Around and Through Female Ambivalence

"What matters it how far we go?" his scaly friend replied.
"There is another shore, you know, upon the other side.
The further off from England the nearer is to France—
Then turn not pale, beloved snail, but come and join the dance.
Will you, wo'n't you, will you, wo'n't you,
will you join the dance?
Will you, wo'n't you, will you, wo'n't you,
wo'n't you join the dance?

...from Alice's Adventures in Wonderland by Lewis Carroll

It has been said that a it is a woman's prerogative to change her mind. Every privilege can be overworked and some men will claim that when it comes to women this is one of them. There is more here than meets the eye especially if the female who strikes your fancy isn't sure she fancies you. The truth be known, you have here a tailor made opportunity for you to use your male energy to win your chance to get to know her.

Every good in nature becomes less desirable when it is over done. This is especially true of personal qualities. For some men there is the risk that in working too much at being masculine they will become emotionally insensitive. It takes a little more work to see the down side of feminine excess. Many women get lost in their intuitive emotions and become cloud borne. Their search for meaning hops from feeling to feeling and they arrive nowhere. When this happens they feel spacy and lost. At such moments they will want you to pull them in. Women want men to solve the problem of their ambivalence. Rescuing them from their uncertainties appeals to them on a number of levels.

Chapter 5 noted the wisdom of persistence and how it makes appeal to a woman's need to watch you discover her. The efforts involved in persisting also send her proof of your trustworthiness. It also pays to persist with an ambivalent woman that you want to get to know. The key is to power through their ambivalence. To power through means what it says—keep on keeping on. Do it nicely because you don't want powering through to become plodding through. Persevere in trying to disperse the mist of her ambivalence with your good resolve to get to her. They will greatly admire your male decisiveness at such times. The idea is to pleasantly put your male fixedness before them.

This does not mean you should be sycophantic and to become a nagging presence. It suffices to let them know gently and softly that your interest is sustained. They will be very pleased to take in the definiteness of your intention. Unconsciously they will try to clone the way of your male energy and put it to work on themselves. This creates a great advantage for you because your magic falls off with your distance from them. It will not take long for her to sense that your advances are making her earth borne again and she will seek the good of your company—with rewards for you in mind, of course.

Powering through a woman's ambivalence is a sophisticated technique. It requires you to see her ambivalence and to make good judgments about where it is and when it is lifting. You should spend time considering when you want to use it. There is some risk of courting a narcissistic personality who will feed endlessly on watching you knock yourself out. Be vigilant for a woman who likes your persistent labors too much. A good rule of thumb for spotting healthy and reasonable ambivalence is her sincere request that you give her time to think it over, as opposed to her spending more of it watching the proof of your interest.

The method of powering through her ambivalence also works when it comes up in a relationship. Here the meaning of your strength of purpose is different. You want to support her in becoming clear on something of importance between you. If ambivalence still clouds the matter after talking it out accept the state she is in and send her your decisive forces. This does not mean sending her your ideas on outcome. Put in her your feelings of being directed and focused to support her ability to come to a clear view of things from her own perspective. Her intuition will tell her that she needs your ways and she will be highly motivated to take them in.

These thoughts apply to yourself also. Men fall into the quagmire of ambivalence also, though usually not as frequently or as deeply as women. When this happens to you side with your own dominant male tendency to be firm and vigorous. Power through the episode by putting off making a decision and putting in effort to create the clarity of spirit and mood that you wish.

To power through describes a technique from race car driving, as I learned in the Spring of 1992 when I went to test drive a sports car. The salesman accompanied me along a twisted and winding country road which he selected to show off the car. As we approached a 30 mile per hour severe turn he said "Take this turn at 60." I looked at him anxiously and he added "Don't worry, it's a deserted road and the police won't bother you". I replied that I was more worried about winding up in the trees than about the police. He laughed and replied "Just power through the curve by accelerating into it. That's what the car is engineered for". I did what he said and it worked perfectly. As the months slipped by my mind worked over that phrase and I found more and more situations where it applied. Becoming clear again when ambivalent is one of them.

Around and Through Female Ambivalence
Exercise for chapter 15

Part I. Use your imagination and try to conjure up some images to represent the idea of powering through female ambivalence. Use material where male and female energies come together. For example, picture yourself high up on a mountain top, looking out into the distance. Far off you see airplanes skywriting. In time their smoky letters begin to melt into the sky and lose their meaning. Eventually there is little left of the original form but clouds going in different directions. Take this to represent female ambivalence.

From the mountain top put that image out there, say to your left. There is a strong wind blowing from higher in the sky and up to your right. Watch it roll into the sky debris and carry it away. The passing of the wind leaves behind a clear blue sky.

Part II. There are other images you can try, such as representing ambivalence by wood floating aimlessly in water and male directedness by the advent of a strong current which carries it away. More subtly, you could play with how a director whips the unconvincing acting of beginners into showmanship.

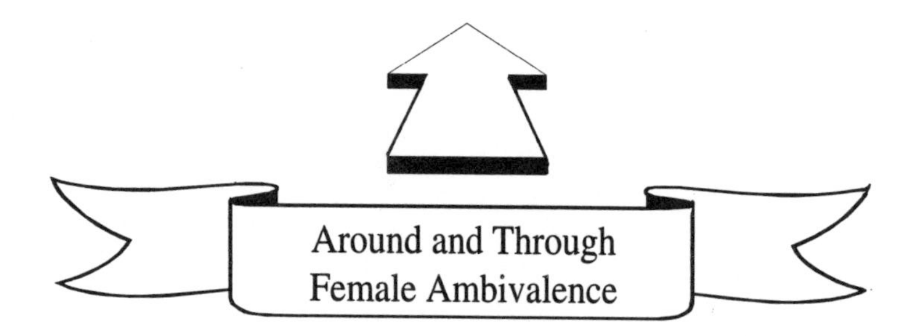

Chapter 16

Wily Women

FIRST WITCH

Round about the cauldron go:
In the poison'd entrails throw.
Toad, that under cold stone
Days and nights has thirty one
Swelter'd venom sleeping got,
Boil thou first i' the charmed pot.

ALL

Double, double toil and trouble;
Fire burn and cauldron bubble.

...from Macbeth by William Shakespeare

Many women resent being referred to as foxes. Their resentment keeps from them how positively it compares them to the striking beauty, elegance and emotional swiftness they share with that creature. Shrewdness and grace are among the many other attributes they share with the wily fox. They also share its stealth. A woman can make her presence known in ways that escape men.

They can send themselves into a crowd with the visibility of a vapor or mist. Other women, however, get their message.

When another woman has eyes for the one she is taken with the message to stay away goes out. Other women pick it up immediately and they may or may not respect its meaning. They may take it as a challenge because women are confident of their ability to win the interests of men from other women. Jealousy comes quickly and strongly to women when another one of them is reaching for the fellow she cares about. A jealous woman has a number of intriguing strategies which she is likely to use. Among the first is to go after the fellow that the other woman really cares about.

This can create a situation you probably won't want to be a part of. She will make herself available and obvious to him (the fellow that the other woman really cares about) and try to draw him in, striking a blow at her real adversary. Be prepared to sense this when it comes your way. Women do not usually make themselves easily accessible to your affections and you should be reasonably cautious when it happens. It is only when you have first won them over with your skill and understanding that this is expectable.

How will you know if her flirtation is the real thing or an act of jealousy? Among the objective signs of her being so interested in you that she will be direct and make it easy for you is the open and honest approach she takes to you. In assuming a basically male approach to meeting she will show signs of the anxieties males experience such as managed, but perceptible concern with the risk taken. Like a man she will sweat over the prospect of rejection but as a woman she will have trouble stifling her much greater concern about not being found desirable. The absence of these two anxieties, and especially the second, is a signal that her motives are questionable. It is very difficult for a woman to put her desirability as a woman on the line.

A similar ploy of a jealous woman is to try to get to the man she really cares about by making herself available elsewhere. Here her jealousy is over his interest in someone else or his lack of sufficient interest in her. Her strategy is basically the same and you should be wary of the signs of insincere interest in you which announce themselves. Those signs are essentially to become too easy to be with and not anxious enough about the outcome.

Women are highly inventive in securing their interests and safeguarding them from others. The virtue of patience runs deep in their makeup and it is admirable. They feel, as noted earlier in chapter 7, that they can wait until their soft and subtle message reaches the fellow she is wishing for. They are usually quietly patient with children and with all phases of growth that need quiet support and love. They are probably more prone to patience when they sense that the man in her life needs some liberty. They almost always grant him an easy liberty from themselves. But there is more in the background.

A woman's love and affection is never without the intent of monogamy and total possession. So while you have your dispensation consider that something else comes with her reasonable affection and tenderness. There is a patient devotion to a larger purpose in her acquiescence to your need for freedom. There is a real existential tension between the tendency of men to long for more freedom and of women to long for more of monogamy.

They will discuss this tension with men with whom they are not involved. They will wish that it were otherwise because monogamy and being there always and ever for that one special man comes so naturally to them. In the end they do what everyone must do to make life work—they make compromises. They concede that they cannot entirely possess a man so they settle for the majority of his life. On their side, men give up some of the need to feel free, whatever that means in any one case, and learn to give more of themselves to her and to show her more devotion. The issue for men is usually to give her more of their emotional life, a thing which makes women feel that men are anchored to them (because that is what it does to them). The issue for women is usually to learn that a man's need for liberty does not mean he is not devoted to them or that he plans to compromise, hurt or abandon the relation. The woman's issue is more difficult than the man's.

Wily Women
Exercise for chapter 16

Part I. This exercise will be easier if there is a jealous woman in your life. If not recall when there was or when you saw one in someone else's life. Go into your visual, auditory and kinesthetic images of her and stay there. What emotional strategies do you see her using to resolve her feelings? Is she making an insincere advance to you or anyone else?

However she manages her jealousy, step into her image and take on her feelings. Do this until it hurts because that's how it feels for her. Deepen the color of the images, turn up the sounds, breathe more deeply and so on, until your pulse quickens as you take on her state. Now ask yourself how you would handle her dilemma. Would you do anything differently or would your solutions be the same as hers? What good things do you find in her state, such as being motivated by tender feelings of affection, wanting to give herself to you and so on?

Part II. Try to part from this experience with a greater empathy for her position in relations. Her good will, like yours, becomes constrained by other peoples' actions. Take your greater awareness with you into your present and future relations.

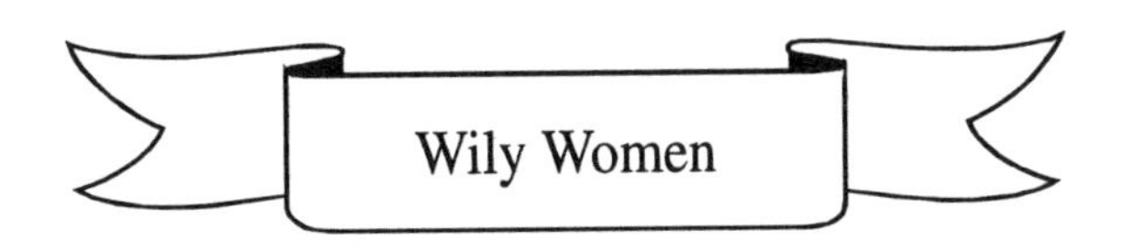

Chapter 17

Playfulness Never Fails

If I am not worth the wooing,
I surely am not worth the winning.

...from The Courtship of Miles Standish
by Henry Wordsworth Longfellow

Every creature in nature has a courting ritual. It tells the other what the first has in mind and invites the other to become a part of it. With women the ritual is a little more complicated. Women carry within their spirits an emotional picture of an ideal flirtation. Favor it and they will favor you. The ritual's expression has playfulness at its center, a thing which makes direct appeal to the heart. Some of its meanings have been noted. For example, a spirit of play disperses the tension at the moment when you first seek her out. It is proof of sorts of the lightheartedness with which you will undertake chances for her sake. In her eyes it also proves your daring do to lift her from her life concerns with your strength and to be there for her. Your sporting appeal to her beauty wins her trust that you have found her from among the others.

Women have frisky instincts. Not just young women, but all women. The wish that men will creatively play with them and remove them from the ho hum of life to levity is always with them. The playful delivery is part of the romantic imagery that they savor. This is what the writers of earlier centuries had in mind when they spoke of women's vanity. It is now called narcissism but it is still there. They want you to tickle their image of themselves and to invite them to run away with you in fancy. They are wonderfully willing to play and some men misread the opportunity as silliness. They have their own bravado and this is one form of it.

They invite you to play before either of you ever says a word. They will look your way for as long as you do not notice them and then they will pretend it wasn't you. Don't believe it. Take up their invitation. If you don't respond they will make themselves more obvious. They will come nearer to where you are. Failing that, they will loiter closer to you and become even more obvious. For the truly dense they have a way that most men never seem to notice but, if you discuss it with them, they will tell you it is so. When all else fails and when they still want you to make the first move, they will take to looking straight at you. They won't look into you, just at you as if to say "Well, come over here".

Playfulness is one of those means that can truly take hold of a woman and sweep her off her feet. It makes such a delightful appeal to their wish to be transported up and away from the present. It offers you the same prospect. The figures of the cavalier, the musketeer and the swordsmen are all expressions of this and they are well worth noting for that information. It is a behavior which is acceptable anywhere, anytime because its appeal is so fundamental.

However, don't rush out to try it at the local supermarket or bakery until you have acquired some skill with it. Study it first in settings which they perceive as socially acceptable such as happy hours, tennis, parties, dances, and so on. As your judgment and skill grows, a thing which you will know by the increase in the fun and success you are having, you can then bring it out into more and more settings. Eventually you will want to use it simply every time you see a women that you want to link with.

I saw a very lovely female placing an order in a bakery recently. I stepped up to the counter near her and heard her say "Make that two blueberry...". I smiled and added playfully in her direction, "Give her three". We looked and smiled at each other and, after I noted her pleasure (which I expected), I took my cue adding with glee "Better make it four". She giggled and laughed and then asked of me, "Well what else do I want to order?" to which I replied with a grin of satisfaction "Whatever you say...as long as I get a part of it". She agreed. This exchange took less than one minute. Play takes hold of women that quickly.

Playfulness Never Fails
Exercise for chapter 17

Part I. Learn to use playfulness to talk to a woman's energy. This is a fun idea and is not the abstraction it may at first sound like. First try to warm up to the idea of it by recalling some times when you were playful as an adult. It's best to recall scenes of playful flirting. Keep the memories in mind and now think of some Hollywood—or other—enactments of flirtation. Sort them out and pick the one you like best. As you reconstruct the scene in your imagination pay special attention to the woman's cues and how the man in the scene picks up on them. Focus on the flow of the speaker role from one party to the other—that's where you find the flow of energy. What feeling is in the cue(s) that the man responds to and vice versa?

Part II. Use your visualization skills to get more in touch with the playfulness by stepping into the man and assuming his actions and feelings. What happens when you do this? Do likewise for the woman and feel her delight over how your performance strikes a chord in her, lifting her up and away. Feel the emotions of reward welling up in her for you. Now go to a recent flirtation from your life, make the appropriate substitutions and repeat the exercise.

Playfulness
Never Fails

Chapter 18

Casting Sexual Spells

I met a lady in the meads
Full beautiful, a faery's child;
Her hair was long, her foot was light,
And her eyes were wild.

...from La Belle Dame Sans Merci
by John Keats

Nothing makes women feel more powerful than to see how their sexuality can rearrange a man. It makes them feel potent. They come to social situations assuming, and rightly so, that men will come to them. They feel in charge of the interaction and in many ways their superior intuitions make it so. At the same time most men are basically well intended and good hearted in their intentions for women. They bring to women a willingness to comply with their wishes in order to gain their affections. In the process many wish that the shoe could be on the other foot, at least some of the time. It seems natural for it to go both ways. It does. Men can undo women just as they undo men.

The ways to get to them are among the most exciting and intense things to be found in life. They are natural expressions of what is masculine and they are easier to do than most men would think. This is one instance where being yourself, and firmly, can pay immense dividends. The actions men need to invest bring words like magnetism, chemistry and passion to this part of life.

Women bring a sense of challenge to your first meeting, just as men do. When they meet you they immediately see your meanings in the way you present yourself—your verbal and nonverbal cues. Some of these tell them how they excite you and some say how delectable your company would be. Give them too much of the first and there is little challenge left for them; you've given the game away, so to speak. It is wiser to prize yourself more and make them work for you. The more you value yourself the more they will. It was once popular to call this being hard to get. It is not just a woman's ploy and, in fact, it improves a man's chances with them more than a woman's.

Women feel a rush of excitement when you draw near. Watch how their shoulders move as you approach them—they cannot hide what you do to them. There is a power in you they are wishing for. It is a power to be closer than they can to risks and even to danger without coming undone. It is a power of self mastery which puts you more in charge of yourself than they can be. It is difficult to exaggerate how much its sense arouses their interest. Every male has it. They cannot feel it and not also feel a rush of sexual excitement with it. Use your emotions and gestures to tell her that you will light up her life with this good stuff if she will show you that she has equally good stuff. The harder she tries to win your interest the more exciting and worthy she will find you.

There is more to the story than show and tell. There is also the delivery. Being sexy is a form of communication. The way you look and move reveals how much in touch you are with your own sexuality and how well you feel about sharing it. Male energy can send a message into a woman telling her how exciting his insides are. You can make a woman wild with excitement by doing this. Do it in a measured way, holding to your need to see her tip her hand, because restraint speaks for your worthiness. It also blunts the prospect of making her feel overwhelmed or undervalued. This is one reason why women like some playful shyness in men—its benign ways can dispel many negative feelings.

The entire process is very fast. The whole thing can put women into a feeding frenzy of interest in only a few minutes. The signals are swapped that quickly. This is all a variant of women's need to be discovered, the variation being that here you don't ask, you demand, so to speak. Your trustworthiness is here also in your ability to withhold your sexuality from her pending more from her—an event which commands instant not-to-be-argued-with respect from her. Women have trouble believing that a man, any man, can say no to an offer of their affections. There is a great deal of mileage in this information.

A woman becomes increasingly vulnerable as her interest mounts. The male who can send himself into her sexual emotions this way can diminish and even shut down the other levels of her needs to be found, to trust, to support and be supported in her purpose. A blindness can come over her so that all her needs collapse into giving herself to this one intoxicating experience. Men can be impulsive at the beginning of a sexual tryst but women can become much more lost to their interest as it grows.

There is a point of theory worth citing on how the meeting of male power and sexuality can spellbind women and simply and utterly put them beside themselves. The energies of the two major drives in man—sexual and aggressive—are not entirely separated. There are points where they become difficult to see as separate and passion is one place where the distinction blurs. Women feel an extraordinary cosmic sense when their arousal draws them so close to a man that they feel his aggressive male energy running together with and into his sexual energy. They begin to merge with men as the men's energies begin to merge with one another. They see themselves unconsciously as setting in motion this great movement of men's energies toward each other.

As for the aggression itself, it seems that they are aroused not by the prospect of being its goal but by its power to make it safe to be near or in danger. Most men know how thrilling it is for a woman to feel that his presence enables her to take risks she would otherwise avoid. Hollywood has worked well an exaggeration of this in the figure of the motorcycle gang.

According to Freud there is an innate masochism at the bottom of women's excitement over male strength. I have known a number of women who, in spite of their feminism and his sexist reputation, agree with him on this. It seems that somehow women like to find pleasure in pain, in at least a few ways. The point can be spelled out more but I think this is clear enough.

His idea makes sense of that most avoidable of women, the "bitch". Her surface behavior seems to have male distress as its goal but what she is really after is provoking the male into doing it to her. Her gains, in Freud's view, are a masochistic pleasure and relief of unconscious guilt. Right or wrong, his ideas are profound and, in my view, worth giving some thought to. As for the figure which they seek to explain, stay away from her. Saucy is one thing but calamity is another.

His notion of female masochism also puts more sense into their longing for you to play with them.

Teasing is a variety of playfulness which appeals to its cousin instinct masochism. Teasing gives them play and some thrilling hints at danger. It also makes some appeal to a wish for some pleasant unpleasure.

Casting Sexual Spells
Exercise for chapter 18

Literature, theater, radio and television are all rich in male figures who possess the smart and swarthy ways described here. Pick some that you feel good about and use the techniques you have learned in previous exercises to master for yourself what they do. As you play out the scenes in your imagination give yourself also to the woman's response. Try to sense not only her excitement but also her dependency and vulnerability in the situation.

Chapter 19

Your Keys

That's the wise thrush;
he sings each song twice over,
Lest you should think he never could recapture
The first fine careless rapture!

...from Home Thoughts, from Abroad
by Robert Browning

This is a natural point at which to pull things together. You have now seen a variety of thoughts, sentiments and methods. They all come together as part of a simple, larger unity. It will serve your purposes well to work on moving toward that higher level of oneness. It is a place where your energy will flow more freely and naturally in the direction you want. That oneness brings ease and completeness to your success.

The next and final chapter bids you bon voyage as a male who self guides to success. You will need to strengthen your command of all the material before we say farewell. This chapter pauses to look back and let you sense more deeply the meanings you have seen. What follows here is essentially an elaborate exercise for as high a level of integration as you wish. It is a very general procedure which you can use to become more thorough with any of the prior material. This exercise may well be the one that you come to enjoy the most and eventually it is likely to be the one that does the most for you. It will make diverse material become so much a part of you that it will come forward on its own to serve you in your quest for success and a richer life.

Select a chapter, any chapter, that you would like to get more out of. Glance through it, note the quotation at its beginning, read it if you wish. Do what you feel you need to capture its spirit and purpose. Become clear on where you want to go further.

Take a look at the circular cluster of words at the end of this chapter. Now place your right hand over them. Let the themes of the material you want to advance with move through you. Choose a part of your right hand to locate a word or group of words. You may feel some definitive sensations in your hand.

Look at the word(s) you chose. For each of them let your images flow into your mind. What ideas and thoughts do they carry? What feelings and emotions do they provoke in you? Let the thoughts and feelings run together. Stay with the experience until you feel satisfied enough to want to move on. Repeat this several times until you feel familiar with your own responses.

Now repeat the procedure with your left hand. The outcome will be different. If you are right handed then the first pass—with your right hand—should put you more in touch with ideas and the second pass—left hand—will stir your feelings and beyond-word sensations. If you are left handed just flip these relations.

Stay with the exercise for a while. Close your eyes and let your right and left hand responses come together in you. Visualize the process with whatever image of the hand responses comes to mind. Watch it until you feel a sense of wholeness. Move on at will to any other chapters you want more from.

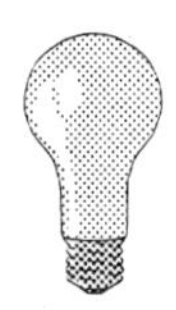
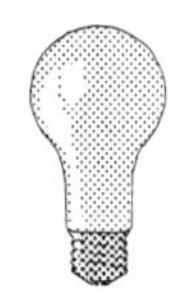

Your Keys

inviting mysterious enchanting
possessive likable creative emotional jealous
challenging flirty spiritual negative nurturing ethereal
sweet patient soft masculine charming haunting lovely
zesty footloose changeable flighty breathtaking ardent airy
feline poetic cosmic lovable ambitious trying passionate
bewitching fair dazzling majestic vain light trustworthy
positive hard successful sexy supportive lithe demanding
demure submissive soulful active intuitive perceptive feeling
difficult exciting voluptuous mesmerizing passive sensitive
heavenly distant radiant aesthetic feminine beautiful
inscrutable magical celestial seductive misty
devilish prepossessing sensuous

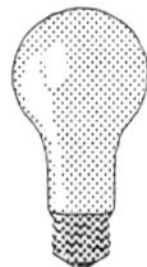

Chapter 20

To Be Your Own Guide

Go, sir, gallop, and don't forget that
the world was made in six days.
You can ask me for anything you like, except time.

...spoken to his aide by Napoleon Bonaparte
From R. M. Johnston, The Corsican

What could be more satisfying and give more grounding to life than having some reasonable measure of self sufficiency. You have seen how to form yourself with images and actions ready to be there for you to create the success you want. I wrote this book with that goal in mind for the reader. Its style and content were chosen to work your feelings and attitudes into effective and energizing directions. That is something you can continue to do yourself, and creatively too. Here are some closing thoughts to bring with you into your life about the momentum of self guiding.

Aristotle once said that well begun is half done. The well begun part here is to hold firmly to some basics which will work for you. Chief among them is to emphasize insight and concept over method. This supports the unfolding of the unique you, a splendid process of living and loving which you should enjoy and pursue with vigor. Methods, in my view, should be studied through the concepts and principles that create them. Done that way, applying and living the method feeds your growth while giving you a useful technique for immediate social gain.

Whether working with insights and ideas or with methods and techniques, the better part of your energies should go into the easy ways of intuition rather than into disciplined and mechanical application of techniques. As you play with the umbrella technique and pick apart what playfulness means and how to do it, go with the flow of emotion and sensation that these things activate in you. When you do that you will naturally and gracefully become more and more creative. You will also be more in touch with the behaviors that beguile women.

The things you pursue are good and wholesome parts of life and nature. It is important to have a sound regard for your goals and to see that you are acting out nature's way. The more you do this the more you will feel nature giving you her energy and putting her wise ways in you. Success is what nature made you for. She made you fully equipped to go from an inner wish, to action to the glow of accomplishment. Part of creating the reality you want is believing in it. The more successful you become the more you will believe in and create the reality you want for yourself.

I chose the quote from Napoleon which begins this section with the luster of his personality in mind. The real Napoleon was a person of sweeping vision and immense commitment. He once wrote to General Lemarois "You write to me that it's impossible; the word is not French." His ambitions only fell short where he interfered with the rights of himself and others. He was otherwise highly successful and that is why France and the rest of the world celebrates him so.

I also chose the quote for its reference to time. Seize the moment and go directly to the things you want. Season your living, loving and doing with the things you have learned. To do that is to do what nature has in mind for you. Here are my good wishes to you to go forward, enlightened, informed and ready to take action to create your success. Bon voyage! Bon appetit!

To Be Your Own Guide
Exercise for chapter 20

Get a pencil or pen and paper. Write down all the social goals that come to mind. Group them into those which you want to achieve first, second and so on. Now go out into life, equipped with your new insight and skill, and create what you want.

Dear reader:

Thank you for reading HOW TO SUCCEED WITH WOMEN. Your comments on it are welcome. Send them to:

Scientific Support
19 Crest Street
Westwood, NJ 07675.

Order additional copies of HOW TO SUCCEED WITH WOMEN by sending $15.00, check or money order, to Scientific Support at the above address or call 201-358-8754 anytime.

Best wishes to you!